FRAGMENTS OF MEMORY

From Kolin to Jerusalem

HANA GREENFIELD

To Lola
Remember!
Hana Greenfield

gefen
publishing house בית הוצאה לאור

JERUSALEM ♦ NEW YORK

Israel 99

Whenever I am faced with documents on the Holocaust, on concentration camps, on mass extermination of Jews by Hitler, on racial laws and on endless suffering of the Jewish people during World War II, I feel strangely paralyzed. While knowing that one must not remain silent, I am desperately speechless. It is as if that paralysis suddenly threw me to the very bottom of the perception of human guilt and of my own co-responsibility for human actions and for the condition of the world in which we live and which we build. It is necessary to talk about the suffering of the Jewish people even though it is so difficult to do so.

President of Czech Republic

Contents

ALICE

Alice was a quiet, shy girl, the only daughter of elderly parents. I was vivacious, lively. In fact, were it not for an unusual set of circumstances, we might never have become friends. We were of the same age, studying in different schools at opposite sides of town. We knew of each other's existence only through brief encounters at the annual Jewish Holy Day services in the only synagogue in town.

And then the world around us started falling apart. British Prime Minister Neville Chamberlain and Herr Adolf Hitler signed a peace treaty that denuded Czechoslovakia of her natural border, the Sudetenland, and no sooner was the ink dry on this infamous document, than the German troops marched into Czechoslovakia and occupied it.

That was the end of our carefree childhood. As one decree after another restricting the freedom of the Jewish population was issued by the Nazi regime, Alice and I got to know each other better.

Schools were closed to us, youth movements like Sokol and Scouts would no longer let us participate in their activities. Our bicycles were confiscated, our musical instruments were taken from us and sent to German youth. We were forbidden to use public transportation or to travel outside our district. Public places, such as swimming pools, tennis courts, movies, theaters and parks, posted new signs announcing that Jews were not wanted there.

Deprived of our normal daily activities, of our school friends, of the freedom of movement we were used to, Alice and I became friends. At first a little shy and awkward, we would meet in different private homes, where clandestine activities for Jewish youth were organized, away from the watchful eye of the Gestapo agents. As we became closer, we would arrange to meet in our homes to study together.

We were so different – two worlds apart! I liked boys, Alice liked books. I loved clothes, Alice loved music. I liked sports of any kind, Alice liked walking by the river Elbe running through our town. Because our lives became so restricted, we compromised our desires and spent many happy hours together, confiding in each other the fears that were descending upon us like heavy clouds. Our dreams of a brighter future boosted our morale, while a yellow star shone from our clothing and our former schoolmates avoided looking at us whenever they would pass us in town.

Meanwhile, the Jewish population of Czechoslovakia was systematically deported to unknown destinations, and town after town became judenrein (free of Jews).

On the 13th of June, 1942, the third and last transport left our town with a cargo of 750 Jews, Alice and I among them. She helped her ailing parents, while I stayed close to my mother, sister, grandmother and aunt. It was frightening leaving with just one suitcase containing so little of our possessions, leaving everything behind in our homes as though we were coming back the next day.

But at the same time it was exciting to leave home on a train, leading to an unknown destination – two curious, frightened and brave little girls who had not yet celebrated their sixteenth birthdays.

Transport List *Yad Vashem Archives*

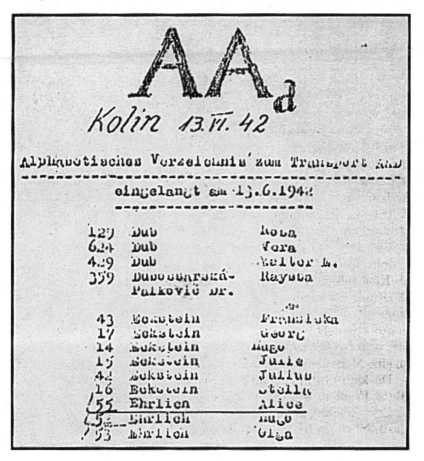

The train arrived outside the Ghetto Terezín in a place called Bohusovice. There, fifty people were taken off the train. They marched, luggage in hand, into the ghetto – among them my mother, sister and I. The remainder of the transport was sent on to the East, its destination unknown to this day. No one returned and no one knows how they perished.

The only thing that remains of Alice is my memory of her and the number "AAd 55" next to her name on the transport list that found its way to the archives of the Yad Vashem museum in Jerusalem.

SAYING GOOD-BYE...

As we are reaching the Golden Age and don't want to be remembered by our children only by the mess we leave behind, I started cleaning up my old files. And there, one day, I came across a forgotten letter, written to me by a friend, a blue-eyed blackhaired girl by the name of Vera. This letter has its own history. It was written after my last visit to Prague, a very exciting trip for a fourteen-year-old girl traveling by herself to visit her girlfriend in 1941. It was also risky as I bravely took off my yellow Star of David, bought myself a ticket and boarded a train, at a time when Jews could no longer travel on public transportation without a Gestapo permit. Our town, under the watchful eyes of the Gestapo, was a very restrictive place for a child who was born and grew up in freedom.

When our time came to be deported from our home, I carefully packed the few things that were dear to me, including Vera's last letter. A couple of years later, when I was forced to leave the Ghetto for my next destination, I left all these little memorabilia with my sister, who remained in the Ghetto. That was fortunate, because in the indescribable world of Auschwitz, we were denuded of all possessions – a photograph of mother, a little love letter, a favorite poem, even our own hair.

After my liberation from Bergen-Belsen, I returned home where I was reunited with my sister and found the last few articles I left with her. These were the only possessions tying me to my past. I read Vera's letter again and cried for this beautiful friend who never had a chance to live and never came home. I took her letter with me when I left for England soon after the war, and later to Israel when I made aliya. Many years later, when I reread her letter I understood that Vera knew she was not going to come back. This is what she wrote me in her last letter:

> 13 May, 1942
>
> Dear Hanka,
>
> Forgive me for not confirming receiving the money for the shoes I purchased for you, you must not be angry with me, because this is the last letter I am writing to you. We have been called for deportation. Six o'clock in the morning the bell rang. I jumped up because I am nearest to the hall, sleeping in the kitchen in the overcrowded apartment. Uncombed and in pyjamas, I looked through the peephole and saw a man with a star standing outside. "Is Mr. Kraus in?" asked the man. There were 400 families by the name of Kraus living in Prague at that time. I must have lost my head for a moment, for I left the man with the star standing outside, until he asked timidly: "Can I come in?" Suddenly, I realized: THIS IS IT!
>
> "Transport?" I asked. By then my parents were up already, and we never went back to sleep again. Let me tell you, it is a different world when you find yourself

Milá Hanko!

Především se Ti musím omluvit,
že Ti tak dlouho nepotvrzuji ty
prachy. Nesmíš se zlobit
stejně ...

ÚSTŘEDNÍ KARTOTÉKA – TRANSPORTY

22376

Krausová Věra

16.3.1926

Praha XII Mánesova 84

1. transport   2. transport
15.V.42   17.5.1942
                    Au-951
Au-1-951   LUBLIN

... Isbica ...
... spíše Isbica dobře char-
akterisovaná. Jíme jako o Jomkipur,
oblečeni jako o Purim a spíme jako o Sukes.
Všichni z Terezína jdou do Polska.

Vaše

Vitka.

Deportation to an unknown destination   *Otto Ungar*

in a transport. In the Jewish community, everybody is asking: "Are you in this one? Leaving? When?" I went to say good-bye to my teacher. She could not grasp that we were being deported. Later, I accompanied my father to the Jewish Community Center to find out what we had to do, what we were allowed to take with us, and a few other errands. We don't know what awaits us, but I am not painting a rosy picture for myself. I know I am leaving for misery, dirt and hunger. A postcard from our friends who left a month ago arrived from Izbice in Poland. They described Izbice as follows: "We eat like on Yom Kippur, we sleep like on Succot and we dress like on Purim. Everybody who arrives in Terezín Ghetto leaves for Poland."

I am really sorry we will not see each other any more. We are entering the quarantine on Thursday at 8 in the morning. Remember me sometimes – "the mischievous Verka" – now I am no longer like that. My mood has changed, but in the afternoon I am going to meet my friends, maybe for the last time, and they will cheer me up a little.

In the meantime I am getting used to the thought of leaving, even looking forward to see all my friends and family who are already there, including my boyfriend Harry.

Let me wish you to walk the path of happiness and freedom in the new shoes and remember your friend, Vera.

Vera Kraus
Transport Au-1, 951

GRANDFATHER

The story I am about to tell mirrors a part of our life in the Ghetto Terezín (Theresienstadt), in Czechoslovakia, during World War II.

The people who were young in the ghetto recall life there with nostalgia, especially in retrospect, after having been in camps such as Auschwitz, Hamburg, Gross Rosen, Bergen-Belsen and others. For the old people it was a different story.

Soon after my arrival in Ghetto Terezín in 1942, it was my good fortune to find work in a kitchen that prepared food for 10,000 people from the meager supplies allocated to the ghetto prisoners by the Germans. To work in any place near food was everyone's dream in the camps.

One day, as part of my kitchen duties, distributing food to the inmates in the Kaserne yard, barracks built in 1878, inside a fortress the Germans turned into Ghetto Terezín, I stood by a barrel of watery soup, ladling the insipid liquid to lines of people queuing in front of me for many hours.

An old man standing before me whispered: "Miss, please give me from the bottom, I am so hungry," hoping that there would be a potato or turnip at the bottom of the barrel. When I looked up, I

Grandfather

recognized the old man as my grandfather. Not wishing to humiliate him, I refrained from making any sign of recognition.

That same day, while cleaning the kitchen, I stole two boiled potatoes. I hid them in my brassiere and managed to smuggle them out of the kitchen, in spite of the body searches made on us every time we left the premises.

Immediately after work I ran to visit my grandfather in the small room he shared with many other old men. I sat down next to him on a straw mattress on the floor, which was the area allocated to him for his *Lebensraum* (living space).

I handed my grandfather the two boiled potatoes I had stolen. He took out a pocketknife, peeled the potatoes, cut them in slices and shared the portions with me. We looked at each other with a smile and felt like conspirators. That was a moment of happiness we shared amidst the sad realities of our daily life in the ghetto.

The following day after work, I rushed to see my grandfather again. Upon entering the room, I discovered he was nowhere to be found. When I asked the others where he was, they replied, "He is no more!"

With the same penknife he had used only a day before to peel the stolen potatoes, my grandfather had cut the veins on his wrist to end his unbearable existence.

When the past becomes a dim memory and the future holds no hope, his was the only free choice. Heroism demonstrates itself not only when we fight with guns; there is also heroism in fighting with what is left to us.

I will always remember my grandfather as one of the unknown heroes of the Terezín Ghetto.

PEN PALS

His name was Michael Mahler. He was from the family of the famous musician, Gustav Mahler. How exactly they were related I never found out, as our brief encounters were so loaded with emotion that there was no time for lengthy discussions. We met in unusual times, full of fear and uncertainty. Yet we were more aware of ourselves than of the dark clouds gathering over us on the political horizon of Europe, like the seed of a pea pushing its way above ground and blooming despite everything.

When the war started and we, the Jewish children, could no longer attend school, partake in extracurricular activities or travel freely, because of the anti-Jewish laws, the Jewish community arranged for pen-pals. That gave us an outlet for pent-up frustrations, a chance to get to know how other youngsters fared under similar circumstances, and provided information on what was happening in other Jewish communities in Czechoslovakia.

The first letter I received was from a young boy at a *Hachshara* (preparation for immigration to Palestine). He wrote that he was a Zionist, that he spoke some Hebrew, which he was learning rapidly, as he wished to be able to speak the language when he made *Aliya* to Palestine.

I reread the letter several times and wondered about the meaning of the words "Zionist," "Hachshara" and "Aliya" and was not at all certain that this boy was the right pen-pal for me.

As a child of patriotic, assimilated Czech Jews, I looked with suspicion at somebody who was ready to abandon his country. But having been well brought up, I felt obligated to answer his first letter. I wrote about my family, about my town which was built in the time of Charles IV, about the river Labe that made its way through the town, where I would go swimming in the summer and ice-skating in the winter. I wrote about the restrictions that were imposed on us by the German occupiers and about the hopes I had to study when normal life would return.

Our next letter exchange revealed curiosity on both sides. We wanted to know how the other looked, how old we were and what school we used to go to. In the following letter we exchanged photographs. In the snapshot that arrived, Michael was leaning on a shovel, dressed in odd-looking work clothes. He appeared tall, slim and good-looking. I felt a little awkward sending him my picture, taken by a local photographer as was the fashion then, in my new *Rosh Hashana* coat, made to order by the best tailor in town, with matching shoes, hat and handbag.

Meanwhile, at home, Jewish women were forced to work in factories, men on the roads. Food was very scarce. We were left without means to buy the little food that was available, as our possessions were systematically confiscated and our bank accounts blocked.

Then another letter came from Michael. He wrote that his group had been dissolved and he was being sent home. Since for every journey a Jew needed a permit from the Gestapo, and while the train was passing through my town, Michael received permission to stop overnight, so we could meet for the first time. With my mother's consent I waited excitedly to get to know my pen-pal.

And Michael arrived – thin, tired and hungry. A beautiful boy with dark hair and blue eyes shaded by endless black lashes, shy, with a charming smile that showed his perfect teeth. I fell in love immediately.

We sat and talked all night. In the early hours of the morning Michael had to leave on the only train going to his town. When we parted, Michael bent down to kiss me. That kiss burned on my lips for a year, until our next encounter in Ghetto Terezín. I was 15 years old.

Suddenly I became aware of the war raging around us. I listened to stories of anti-Semitic attacks from people that had to leave their homes in Sudetenland and came to look for shelter in our community. I heard the shrill voice of the Führer and his tirades on the Jews on the radio and trembled with fear.

Under SS Obergruppenführer Reinhard Heydrich, the "Protector of Bohemia and Moravia," the situation worsened daily for us Czech Jews. Slovakia proclaimed itself an independent state; Poland fell. Germany occupied Denmark and invaded Norway and Holland capitulated to the Germans.

As town after town was cleared of Jews being deported to unknown destinations, my family started to prepare itself for a similar fate. The day came only too quickly. After Heydrich's assassination by two Czech partisans in Prague, the Germans sent off a "penalty transport" from my home town. At the Bohusovice railway station the train stopped. Fifty persons were taken off the train and marched, luggage in hand, into the Terezín Ghetto, a journey of three kilometers. The rest of the passengers on the train continued their journey, never to be seen or heard from again.

In Terezín I worked and waited. I waited for the Jews of Michael's town to arrive in the ghetto. After a year, a transport from Hradec Kralove, where Michael lived, arrived, and his name was on the list. We, the ghetto inhabitants, were not permitted to meet the new arrivals. Only when they were brought inside a large hall called *"Schleuse"* did I manage to slip in.

And there was Michael! Our eyes met and we awkwardly shook hands. Michael introduced me to his parents. A gray-haired lady and a sick man in a wheelchair. Since I worked in the kitchen, I brought along some food I had stolen. They were embarrassed by my gift. They did not yet know what hunger was, and I no longer knew what it meant not to be hungry.

The next time I managed to visit them I found Michael lying on a thin mattress placed on the floor, burning with high fever. His mother was having a hard time coping with a sick son and a disabled husband. It took a couple of days until a doctor was found and brought to see Michael, who was diagnosed as having an inflamed appendix. With a little stolen sugar I bribed someone to have Michael transferred to one of the ill-equipped hospitals in the ghetto.

Since I worked a night shift and then slept through the day, it was not until two days later that I could visit him in the hospital, only to be told that Michael was being operated on, and I was not permitted to see him.

The next day a friend working in the hospital as a nurse came running to tell me that Michael had died during the night of a ruptured appendix, and the funeral was to take place in a few hours.

In a daze I arranged to be relieved from my work and in haste made my way to the mortuary that resembled a factory. Tens of wooden boxes were piled on top of each other, names were being called rapidly, a Rabbi was saying *Kaddish*, the traditional Jewish prayer for the dead.

Michael's mother and I walked together behind the hearse, piled with wooden coffins, pulled by prisoners up to the gate, from where only the dead had the privilege to leave the ghetto. We were strangers, but our love for Michael and the pain of losing him brought us unbelievably close. I gave Michael's mother our pen-pal letters and we said goodbye, never to meet again. That was on a cold morning, January 7, 1943.

It was I who fulfilled Michael's aspirations. I survived the concentration camps, made Aliya and became a Hebrew-speaking Zionist in my own free country, Israel.

The Last Journey   *Pavel Fantel*

ntgetthoisiert"

AUSCHWITZ

Entering Auschwitz was like entering a Gate to Hell. No matter how conditioned we were to suffering in the previous camps, nobody was prepared for the visual horrors and harsh treatment that greeted us there.

Arriving at night, tired, hungry and thirsty, searchlights pointing at us, a barbed wire fence surrounding us, we could not see where our luggage was, or where the next blow would come from. Fear propelled us to continue.

From the first moment of arrival, we were pushed by blows and shouts to evacuate the stinking overcrowded wagons that had brought us there. Some of the prisoners, forced to receive us this way, were friends who had arrived by previous transports to Auschwitz. All this was carried on under the watchful eyes of the SS officers supervising the operation, accompanied by vicious, barking dogs.

My stay in Auschwitz was a nightmare. This was a different world, a place with a life of its own. Here, time was measured by endless *Appells* (roll calls), the inmates having to stand twice a day to be counted over and over again, because by the time the counting was finished, there were always a few dead bodies confusing the SS, so intent to be exact in their task.

In Auschwitz, time had different dimensions. The outside world, where everything was measured exactly by time, where watches and clocks and calendars were a framework to daily life, seemed far away and foggy in our Auschwitz life. Time here was defined by waiting for the one daily ration of a slice of bread and a bowl of watery soup, which did not always arrive.

People that lived there had no names, just a number branded on their arm, a big hole in their belly filled with hunger, and a shaved head full of fear. In Auschwitz the birds didn't sing, flowers didn't grow, people were not born, they only died there.

Auschwitz was German ingenuity combined with talent for

"Appell"   Mieczyslaw Koscielniak

organization that had created the ultimate killing machine, and we became its programmed victims.

We were spectators and victims of a monstrous nightmare from which we could neither awaken nor escape.

While watching the chimney belch out the red smoke, like the last breath of a choking man, with the sweet smell of burning flesh permeating the air, I cried out in desperation: "G-d, where are you?"

Selection of Women   *Jerzy Potrzebowsky*

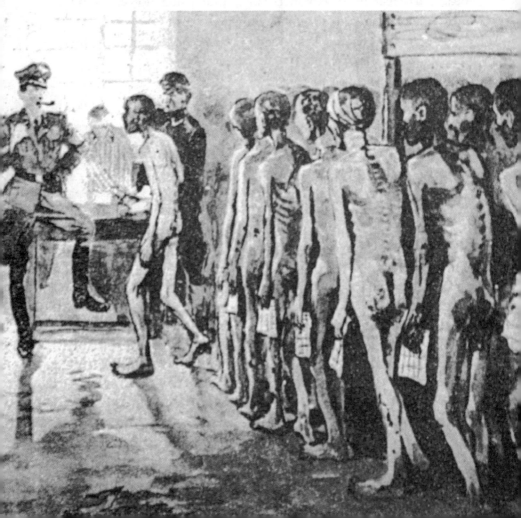

THE LAST BOWL OF SOUP

The inscription read: "To the Night Butterfly at No. 112, from Esti. Terezín 15.X.1942." It was on the reverse side of an old photograph that miraculously survived, of a young girl in a white blouse. She brings back memories I must commit to paper before they disappear.

In the fall of 1942, Terezín's overcrowded army barracks were opened up; until then, all the inmates of the ghetto had been accommodated in them. The houses of the original inhabitants of Terezín town, forcibly transferred to other places, became available to us, the prisoners of the ghetto.

I found a small room in an old house, No. 112, which I shared with twenty other women. Here we put down our mattresses and our few belongings on the bare floor and enjoyed relative privacy in comparison to the halls we had lived in, where 300-400 people were packed together.

Transports with new prisoners were constantly arriving from all over *"judenfrei"* Europe, filling up every available space in the ghetto. One day a new girl, tall and slim and a little frightened, moved into our room. We, the oldtimers, tried to make her comfortable by pushing our mattresses closer together, making space for hers.

She and I were close in age, both 16, both lonely among so many, and we soon became friends. We commiserated together about the ghetto conditions, talked with nostalgia about our homes and families, about our first love and how it felt to be kissed for the first time. We were young, with a will to live, and hope for a better future sustained us in our dreary daily life, while our stomachs continually rumbled from hunger.

I soon found work in a large kitchen that provided food to thousands of prisoners from the meager supplies allocated by the Germans. It was hard physical labor. However, I was no longer hungry, as my fingers always found their way into the pot. Sometimes I even managed to organize (we never called it stealing, as we were not thieves, just hungry) a delicacy of burned flour, sugar and margarine mixed together, a sheer delight that I would bring home and share with my new friend, Esti.

We met early in the mornings when I returned from night duty and before she left for her work, and again in the evening, when she returned and I was just about to leave. That is how I came to be called "night butterfly."

Soon after we met, I contracted typhus and was taken with high fever to an isolation hospital where I fought for my life for three months. In the meantime, with all the upheavals in the ghetto, transports coming and others going to unknown destinations, each carrying another family member or friend, Esti and I lost sight of each other.

In 1944, I was sent with many others to Auschwitz and there, in this indescribable hell, we met again. A few weeks after my arrival, as I began to become accustomed to this non-existence that we

„Nočnímu motýlkovi" na čísle
112
věnuje Edi. Jedlín, 15.X. 1942.

lived through, I discovered that Esti was in the same camp in a "hospital" that was not equipped to heal the sick.

It was a large building with three-tiered bunkbeds filled with half-dead human beings, without medicine, sheets or any comfort one would associate with the concept hospital. No inmate ever wanted to end up there, as Auschwitz was not kind to sick people.

There I found Esti lying in one of the bunkbeds – in the middle tier, skin and bones, her face just two large eyes – wanting to jump out and run, run away from here even though her body was no longer able to do so. Whenever the opportunity presented itself, I would try and visit Esti, sit next to her, sometimes feed her with the watery soup that came once a day, sometimes wash her with a little rag and water I brought with me in a tin pot, wiping away some of the blood she spat out.

On my last visit, I found her mother sitting on her bed. Esti was terribly weak and could no longer talk. Covered with a thin grey blanket which served to outline the contours of her childlike body, she was having difficulty breathing. Just then the daily ration was being distributed, and her mother took Esti's tin pot to stand in line for the soup. When I looked at Esti, her eyes were open, still, no longer shining. I touched her hand and it fell out of mine.

When her mother returned with the soup, she realized that Esti had left us. She sat down on the edge of the bed, ate Esti's last soup ration, got up, closed Esti's eyes, covering her face with the thin grey blanket. Then she sat down and cried...

Barrel of soup ▶
Dinah Gottlieb

PUNISHMENT

Erna will always remain my heroine. How many times I asked myself, how would I have taken such heavy punishment? Would I have screamed? Cried? Told anything they wanted to know? Which blow would have been the breaking point? The fifth? The tenth? Would I have survived or remained sane?

Erna was born and brought up in Hamburg, Germany. When evacuation of German Jews was on the agenda, Erna was deported to Ghetto Terezín in Czechoslovakia. When the over-crowded ghetto was being prepared for a Red Cross visit and transport after transport left the ghetto, Erna was placed in one destined for Auschwitz.

At that time, a decision was made by the Nazi government in Berlin to stop killing able-bodied Jews. The Germans realized they needed every hand to continue feeding their war machine. From then on selections were made in Auschwitz and prisoners that passed the test were for the first time in Auschwitz history sent to slave labor all over the German Reich.

Erna and I were among the 500 women that left the hell of Auschwitz and, by a cynical coincidence, she arrived back in her home town, Hamburg, where she had started her sad journey a few years earlier.

Our first incarceration was in Hamburg's port, Freihafen's storage buildings, where ships were loaded and unloaded with the ebb and flow of the river. We women prisoners were sent to differents parts of the city, which was under daily bombing, to clean up the rubble so that civilian life could continue in Hamburg.

Returning from work one day we found Freihafen bombed out and were transferred to a different camp in Neugraben, another suburb of Hamburg. Again we were distributed to different places to work wherever the Germans could use us Jewish slaves.

It was in a brick factory that blond Erna caught the eye of one of the German workers who seemed to be a little more human and sympathetic than the rest of our guards. In time this man agreed to take a letter to her sister, who remained in Hamburg, being married to a Gentile. The day the man brought a small parcel of clothing and food for Erna from her sister, an SS patrol paid our work place a visit and the parcel was discovered. After some interrogation, it was established that it belonged to Erna.

Returning to our Neugraben camp, we were not allowed to receive our customary meager portion of soup. Instead, we were called immediately for an *appell* (roll call) and left standing for hours in the open, while Erna was being interrogated in the Lagercommandant's office. Finally, she was brought outside by two SS women. The 500 women, her co-sufferers, were forced to watch her punishment.

Our Lagercommandant, Spiez, in his smart uniform and highly polished boots, with a whip in his hand and a few armed SS men in tow, forced Erna to bend down and started whipping this defenseless girl. We, the unwilling witnesses, were frozen to the ground by fear, humiliation and the shame of not being able to help. We listened in silence to the swishes of the whip and the screams that never left Erna's lips. As the force of the whippings

escalated, foam formed around the mouth of the Lagercommandant and when he reached his climax, with Erna on the
ground, he left.

The girls picked up Erna, brought her inside the barracks where
one of us, a doctor, took care of her as best as possible under the
circumstances. Erna never revealed the name of her sister nor the
man that helped her. She slowly recovered.

When our next camp, Tiefstak, was bombed out by the Allies,
we were again transferred elsewhere. During an exceptionally
heavy raid on the railway line that was taking us to Bergen-Belsen,
Erna escaped.

Fifty years later, her silent screams continue to wake me from
my nightmares.

Painting by German pupil from the town of Neugraben   *Helms Museum*

HAMBURG, CHRISTMAS 1944

It is still dark outside. I lie on the bunk bed and wonder why I am up so early. Is it the cold that disturbs my sleep? I crawl into myself and my thin body becomes a little bundle, like a baby in its mother's womb. The short, threadbare grey blanket barely covers me. Another prisoner must have torn a piece from its end, probably to create makeshift gloves to protect her hands from frostbite. Suddenly somebody switches on the light, the glare hurting my eyes. We don't have any watches – those were taken away from us a long time ago – but it must be about five in the morning. I peek out from under the cover to see a young SS Sturmbannführer. I don't know his name, he never introduced himself to us. He is tall, blond and blue-eyed and, with a bucket of cold water in his hand, he screams his new daily curse in a perfect Hamburg accent, emphasizing the "S" in *"Schweinehunde aufstehen!"* (Pigs, get up). And with a laugh he pours the icy water over us girls lying terrified in the bunkbeds.

After that, it doesn't take too long to get dressed. Anyhow, we only owned one piece of clothing, a prisoner's uniform that most of us took off only in order to get washed when and if we had the opportunity. I climb down from the upper deck, where, luckily, not

Returning From Work   *Dina Gottlieb*

much of the cold water had reached me. Searching under the bed for my pair of wooden clogs, I find that someone had decided during the night that I should share them with her. With one clog on and the other foot wrapped in an old newspaper tied with a string, I am ready for the day's work.

Morning toilet is very simple. No toothbrush, no toothpaste, no comb, no soap. And already we have to stand at Appell. We have to be counted. Whether leaving or entering the camp, we must always be counted, for we, the women slaves, are very precious to the Third Reich. Morning cold penetrates right through our thin clothing and we start to shiver. "Nu," I think to myself, "it is better to start marching already than to stand and freeze to the ground."

Finally the columns move out of the camp. We never know our destination, or who our next employer will be. We go out every morning, some to clean up the rubble of the bombed out buildings on the streets, others to replace railway lines that were blown up the previous night or to dig frozen ground, in order to repair damaged water pipes. Some also work in brick factories.

We work all day under the supervision of SS men and SS women dressed in their green uniforms. They come in pairs. They sit around guarding us; they talk and laugh, eat and drink, and when they become bored, they hit us.

Sometimes when we get permission to relieve ourselves, we run to see if there is anything to eat. Maybe a rotten apple under a tree, maybe some potato peels in the garbage. It has to be quick so that the "green ones" don't miss us.

Suddenly the now familiar sound of wailing sirens interrupts the monotony of the work. The "green ones" are frightened; they run for cover in deep bomb shelters. We are left alone in the open field. Now we can rest, we can stop working, because nobody is watching us for a while. It doesn't take a minute before a deafening sound is heard. Not far off, a building is blown up. An airplane explodes like a star in the sky. Then all is quiet again and the "green ones" come back.

It is beginning to get dark when we return to camp through Hamburg's suburbs. Through the windows of the houses we can see decorated Christmas trees in every living room. It all looks so inviting, so warm and so beautiful. It all seems so abnormal in our dreary prisoners' life.

Walking wearily in the snow, dragging one tired foot after the other, I become lost in my thoughts: "It would be nice to be a Christian just for one evening. To warm up my frozen feet in that cozy lit living room, to fill my hungry, shrunken stomach with some warm food and maybe fall asleep in a real bed?"

"Marsch, marsch! Schnell, schnell!" the SS women guards start screaming at us, for they also want to get back to the camp. It is Christmas eve!

Hungry, dirty and exhausted, we reach the gate of the camp in the dark. After another roll call and a body search, a ration of bread and a bowl of watery soup is received by whoever has the strength to stand in line for it. Another day ends.

HEILIGE NACHT... STILLE NACHT... HOLY NIGHT... SILENT NIGHT...

RIGHTEOUS GENTILES

It was in the midst of a harsh winter in the year of 1944. The days were long and full of suffering. Without underwear, scarves, hats or gloves, the cold penetrated into every part of our bodies. The feet were the worst. Without socks or stockings, our wooden clogs did not protect us from the frost and snow. As we walked to or from our day's work, the snow would stick to the wooden sole and keep building up until we looked like circus performers, hobbling on stilts. We would stop, bang on the sole of the shoe, scrape the snow off, and continue.

After our camp in Freihafen was levelled by bombs, we were transferred to another one in Neugraben. The miserable living conditions did not change, if anything, they became worse. Instead of working clearing rubble from bombed out buildings, we were in the suburbs of Hamburg, repairing frozen water pipes and working in brick and munition factories.

Because we were working in the open countryside, where there were only a few scattered houses, and since there were no toilets, we were allowed, from time to time, to run into the surrounding area to relieve ourselves among the trees and bushes.

One day, while out of sight of the SS men and women who guarded us, I mustered all my courage and knocked on the door of a house – its chimney puffing smoke into the cold grey air.

After the second knock, an old woman opened the door, bewildered at what she saw, but no more frightened than I, while words pleading for food came out of my mouth. The woman, after a few moments of hesitation, during which I nearly died of fright, beckoned me in. Guiding me into her kitchen, she spoke briefly to her husband, who sat in a corner repairing shoes. She took out a soup bowl and poured some hot liquid into it. I ate in haste, not wanting to be missed by the guards, for punishment for such a breach of discipline was harsh. I thanked them both and ran. As I was leaving, the old lady whispered to me, "Come again when you can."

A couple of days later, while working at the same site, I managed to slip away. This time I knew my destination. Eagerly, I knocked on the door of the same house, with the nostalgic memory of having my shrunken stomach filled with the delicious liquid of my previous visit.

Again, it was the old woman who opened the door carefully. Upon seeing the same hungry girl in a torn striped uniform with wooden clogs on her feet, she let me in quickly. After serving me a bowl of sweet thick porridge, she murmured something to her husband and handed me an old pair of men's shoes with new soles that her husband had prepared for me. The shoes were twice the size of my feet, but with old newspaper stuffed inside, I fitted them to my frozen feet and tied them up with string. I thanked them for this priceless gift, and although I would have liked to linger in their warm kitchen a little longer, fear propelled me on. I ran in my new warm shoes, my feet slowly defrosting in all that vacuum, no longer wet from the snow. The guards noticed neither my absence nor my new acquisition.

The next day we were sent elsewhere to work and never again returned to that neighborhood. I never learned the names of those good people nor their address, but for the rest of the winter I blessed them, while my frozen feet recovered thanks to their kindness and humanity. These were righteous gentiles.

When Abraham spoke to God in order to save Sdom from destruction, God answered him: "If you find ten righteous people among its inhabitants, I will save the city." (Genesis 18:32)

In the difficult days I lived through in Hamburg during the war, I found two good people who restored my faith in humanity and made it possible for me to return there again, many years later, at the invitation of the Mayor of Hamburg.

THE FIFTEENTH OF APRIL, 1945

April 15, a date forever engraved in my memory. If I mention it to someone today, many years later, a blank expression comes across their faces. What is so special about it? It was the day of our Liberation!

How many times did we dream about this day? In how many different ways did we imagine it? It was the hope of living to this day that sustained us.

We were 500 Czech women, carefully selected by the SS to be sent for slave labor in Germany, the first transport ever to have left behind the gas chambers and the smoking chimneys of Auschwitz.

It was only when we arrived in Hamburg, the large port city of Germany, and were housed in Freihafen – storage buildings being bombed day and night by the Allies – that we realized it wasn't the goodwill of the Germans that had brought us out of Auschwitz. And then I understood the stories my Rabbi had taught me: We had become slaves, just like the Jews in Egypt in Moses' time.

For more than a year we slaved under unbearable conditions, witness to the destruction of Hamburg by the American bombers by day and the British bombers by night. The daily attacks took their toll among us slave laborers as well.

Bergen-Belsen 15 April 1945   *The Living Among The Dead*

The German population of Hamburg saw us, marked Jews, as we marched daily to and from work in different parts of the city, wherever our labor could be used to the advantage of the Third Reich.

After our camp was bombed out for the second time and it became impossible to take us to work, we were transported to Bergen-Belsen, a name synonymous with hell.

We arrived at the Bergen railway station in a sorry state. Some of our women had been killed and others wounded by an accurate attack on the rail line. Bedraggled, we looked a pitiful sight.

From Bergen we were forced to walk to Belsen. The road was full of dead bodies, thrown to the side, of those who had gone before us on their last walk. Some dropped dead, some were shot when they could no longer continue the death march. No sooner did we reach the camp than the panicked Germans loaded onto us, like donkeys, the contents of their warehouses and, prodding us with guns and blows, forced us to march back to Bergen. More trains were arriving with similar human cargo, under the same inhumane conditions, from other camps in Germany. We were hungry, we were thirsty, but nobody cared.

Some of our girls fell in the ditch during the darkness, some managed to escape into the woods. Once we were back in the Bergen-Belsen camp, our nightmare began. Whoever lived through the experience of Bergen-Belsen lived through his own death.

Death was everywhere. It stared at us from everyone's eyes. The pitiful "Muselmänner," the walking dead bodies, no longer knew where they were walking to or why. Everyone was searching for non-existent food. Our tongues were swollen from lack of water. The little water that was available was contaminated with typhoid bacilli. Some drank from it, no longer caring.

At night, we heard the guns of the advancing armies from Bremen. How much longer can it take before they reach us? How much strength will it take to stay alive until then?

And then it happened. The first British tank rolled inside the camp, opened the gates of this indescribable hell, and a bull horn sounded the sweet words we had waited for, for so long: "YOU ARE FREE... YOU ARE FREE... YOU ARE FREE... "

Those of us who were still alive – while thousands lay dead, no longer having had the strength or the will to live – became free. And so the Fifteenth of April 1945 will forever remain engraved in my memory.

WHEN MEMORY COMES...

When I came to England, in January 1946, my uncle, who was a gentle man, a doctor of medicine and a brilliant scientist, came to receive me at Croydon Airport. Where the passengers descended the ramp of the plane, a hostess was waiting, asking if there was a child aboard the plane that had just landed from Prague. She had instructions to receive and take care of a child who arrived alone.

When I answered to the name she called out, the ground hostess looked at me and thought some mistake in identity must have occurred. There stood a young lady, well dressed, grown up and very sure of herself.

What a shock this presented to my uncle, who expected a poor, thin, hungry child – a child he remembered from our last meeting at my grandmother's home before the war, in 1938 – ravaged by four years in concentration camps.

Nobody realized in those days that we, the survivors were ravaged in our souls, our emotions, that we were one great pain filling every crevice of our guts. The outside was a camouflage, a protective cover that enabled us to live among normal people. Had the outside resembled the inside, we would have looked like lepers among the others.

This, of course, presented a problem for my uncle, who didn't know how to cope with the unexpected situation. He was a product of a typical Czech Jewish intellectual family, assimilated to the point where being a Jew was the last thing to play a role in his life, until the day Hitler marched into Czechoslovakia in 1939. He was caught unprepared, lecturing at Cambridge University at that time, while his wife and child were left in Prague.

While searching for his mother and his family, he found my name as the only member of a large family on the list of Bergen-Belsen survivors. Out of the kindness of his heart he asked me what he could do for me. My answer came without hesitation: "Please get me out of Europe."

As we sat facing each other there at the airport, I pouring out all the horror of the deportations, the terrible suffering the family had been forced to endure, he gently interrupted me and said: "Please don't talk about it when we get home. I don't want my children to know. And you – try to forget."

Life became very difficult for me in his home. In spite of my outside appearance, I was a raped child. I was robbed of my mother and my father, of my home and of the love and warmth to which every child is entitled. I ached with pain and I wanted to talk about it. I wanted to cry and I wanted to scream, and I wanted to be comforted and hugged and understood. Instead I was told to be silent and to forget. FORGET?

◀ *Upon arrival in England*

BREAD

Walking down the street one morning, I was stopped by the smell of fresh bread. I looked around to see where it came from, and my eyes drew me closer to a window display of the most attractive, delicious-looking French breads, croissants, raisin rolls and black and white breads of every imaginable shape: BREAD!

Once bread was the very substance of my life. A small piece of black bread meant another day of remaining alive. When one is very hungry, it isn't luxury one desires, it is that basic piece of bread which dominates the craving to fill the hole in one's stomach. To ease the pain that crawls into every crevice of the body when food is denied for an extended period of time.

How hungry can one get? We can fast on Yom Kippur. We feel the hunger during the day, but we fill the day with prayers, knowing that, at the end of a limited period of time, there will be relief from this temporary discomfort.

Then there is the hunger of the concentration camps, hunger that is continuous, day after day, when one is never full, never satisfied with the rations so meager as to be tormenting, only marginally stilling the obsessive hunger.

And then, there is the hunger of years of food deprivation, when a human being can hardly concentrate on any subject other than how to find a piece of bread to rid himself of that terrible pain hunger causes, pain that becomes an integral part of one's daily life.

There were strange ways we and bread coped.

What is the price of bread? That depends on the market. Today it may be the minimal few cents, pounds or shekels. There were days when bread had value beyond imagination. A diamond for bread? A friendship for a slice of bread? One's body for bread? What is the value of a life when it no longer has the strength to breathe, to think, to function or to enjoy?

A slice of bread could be eaten in the evening, so that the pain would be somewhat relieved and one could fall asleep for a few hours. Or one could keep one's ration of a slice of bread for the whole of the next day, chew on it slowly through a day of hard labor. Or, falling asleep with exhaustion, hide the bread under one's head, only to wake up finding the treasure gone, stolen by someone else just as hungry.

Hunger is desperation. Hunger is death. A piece of bread will extend life for a day or perhaps a few hours. Gold, money, diamonds – what a laugh! Absurd, worthless, they cannot be eaten!

How can I explain this to my children, while bread is being thrown in the garbage, fed to animals, while everybody tries to eat less bread to keep slim?

I used to have a dream: When this ordeal is over and if I survive it, I want to have ten loaves of bread with me all the time. To see them, to touch them, to nibble on them, forever. That was my vision of paradise. The smell of fresh bread will always bring back these memories.

RETURN TO KOLIN

Searching for facts to confirm my memories, I hesitatingly returned to the country of my birth, to the town and to the very house in which I was born. The day I arrived it rained so hard that it was as if the whole world were crying with me over the sad fate of the Jewish community I had been born into.

Kolin – a charming old town in the heart of Bohemia, 60 kilometers east of Prague. In the Middle Ages, in the time of Charles IV, it had been a walled city with an imposing Gothic church and the second largest Jewish community outside of Prague.

Kolin had a continuous Jewish presence from 1376. The large, jungle-like cemetery in the town dating from 1418 is proof of this fact.

Professor Josef Vavra, in his book published in 1886 on the history of the King's City of Kolin on the river Elbe, writes that, as indeed appears in the town registry, Jews already lived and owned property in Kolin during that time. In 1512 there was also a Jewish school registered and a flourishing Jewish community.

I found our beautiful, large synagogue, with its magnificent stained glass windows, hidden behind an ordinary street entrance in the old Jewish quarter, locked, unused and badly neglected. Yet the Ark was still there, with its Ten Commandments, shining through dimness and the eerie silence.

Closing my tear-filled eyes for a moment, I suddenly heard the rich voice of our cantor, Mr. Reichner, the sermon of my teacher and esteemed Rabbi, Dr. Richard Feder, and the chanting of prayers by the congregants, the children, of whom I was one, running in and out of the synagogue, visiting parents and grandparents and playing outside.

I opened my eyes to the emptiness and to the dead silence and, as I got used to the darkness, I realized that all the chandeliers, which used to light up the synagogue each holiday with their brilliance, were missing. They are now a part of the collection belonging to the Jewish Museum in Prague.

In the steady downpour I made my way to the new cemetery at the other end of the town, over the bridge that spans the river Elbe, to pay my respects to those buried there and to those memorialized in a communal monument erected after the war, their graves unknown.

Even this new cemetery, dating from 1880, is unattended and overgrown, yet so green and peaceful. My grandfather, grandmother and many members of my family are buried there. I found their graves with ease by the imposing black marble tombstones and gold lettering.

The Jewish community of Kolin (including the surrounding villages), under the leadership of Rabbi Dr. Richard Feder since 1917, numbered close to 3,000 Jews.

Until the day, when in reprisal for the assassination of Reinhard Heydrich, Hitler's chief officer of the Protectorate of Bohemia and Moravia, not only the village of Lidice was eliminated, but also 750

Monument erected in Kolin Jewish cemetery after the war

Jews of Kolin were sent to Trawniki, Poland, where they were all murdered upon arrival – a fact never made public.

Only a handful of the others returned from the concentration camps after the war. Dr. Richard Feder, who later became Chief Rabbi of Czechoslovakia, was among them.

Walking through the town, I realized that half the stores had been Jewish-owned. Most of them are still selling the same type of merchandise, but the names of the original owners are no longer there. I passed by my school, where I was the only Jewish child in the class, the playground where I spent many happy hours until the sign "Jews are not wanted here" appeared. I passed the homes of my friends who never returned, the park, the tennis court. It is all there.

It was an eerie experience coming back to my home town, where life continues without the Jews who were for so long part of its history. I felt like a ghost. Leaving town, I wondered how different our fate might have been if the Czech people had stood up for the Jews who for centuries had thought they were an integral part of that nation.

KOLIN... AND A SEFER TORAH

Jewish life was never easy in Kolin – the second oldest Jewish community after Prague. Following the big fire in which the old city of Prague was destroyed, Jews were accused of having cooperated with the Turks in initiating the fire. Having been made the scapegoats, they were expelled under the order of Ferdinand the First. A few years later, Jews were allowed to return, since they were a very positive influence in the fields of commerce and development in the town of Kolin.

In 1634, two officers of the Czar started a fire that burned 40 houses in Kolin. By checking records, I discovered that the house that my grandmother bought in 1900 in Prazska Ulice, located in the center of town and connected with the Jewish quarter, was sold as a burned house in 1635, only a year after the fire.

In 1848, 30 Jews who were members of a unit of the National Guard went to aid the revolution in Prague. Kolin was known for its yeshiva which, in the 19th century, became modernized and was called *"Beth Hamidrash-Anstalt"* (Institution). Moses Montefiore was impressed by it during his first visit in 1885 and endowed a foundation for its students.

Rabbi Dr. Richard Feder

The Jewish community of Kolin also had its share of blood libel. In 1913 a young woman, made pregnant by a Roman Catholic priest, committed suicide. The young priest, named Hrachovsky, tried to implicate the Jews in a blood libel, but fortunately they were ultimately exonerated.

The Jewish presence continued in Kolin. Between the two World Wars, the city was a stronghold of the Czech-Jewish movement. An interesting episode occurred when about 600 Jews organized themselves for collective emigration and were offered the support of the French government in establishing a settlement in New Caledonia, but the project was aborted when World War II erupted.

Between the two World Wars the Jewish community of Kolin prospered and grew under the leadership of Rabbi Dr. Richard Feder. We thought of ourselves as part of the Czech nation, differentiated only by our faith, until the outbreak of the Second World War, when Czechoslovakia was occupied by Germany. As early as January 1940, Jewish shops had already been confiscated and Jewish women – including my sister and myself – were forced to work in the local soap factory, Hellada.

Today the sole remnant of that rich community is an abandoned, decaying synagogue and two graveyards spanning 600 years of Jewish presence there.

The Torah scrolls from Kolin were miraculously preserved in Prague, together with the rest of the collection of ceremonial objects collected by the Germans from each of the 153 disappearing communities, as soon as each one was eliminated. Today they form the largest collection of Jewish ceremonial objects in the world. Some of them are on permanent display in the Jewish Museum in Prague.

The 1564 Torah scrolls, found in Prague after the war as part of the loot seized by the Germans, were acquired by the Westminster Synagogue in London, England. With loving care they have repaired and restored many of them and redistributed them among many synagogues throughout the free world.

One of the Torah scrolls found a new home in the Northwood Pinner synagogue in London, where a symposium was held on how to preserve the memory of the Jewish communities that perished in the Holocaust. To make it meaningful and alive to the present generation, the symposium presented translated letters from the Rabbi, a paper by a student researching a particular chapter in the history of Kolin Jews, and a question and answer panel chaired by a surviving member of the Kolin community – myself.

And so the 25 scrolls from Kolin are scattered today among synagogues from Australia to Israel as the last remnant of that community.

These scrolls will serve as a continuous reminder of the Kolin Jewish community for future generations.

Tiffereth Shalom, Ramat Aviv, Israel

Northwood Pinner Synagogue, Middlesex, England

South London Liberal Synagogue, England

Temple Shir Shalom, West Bloomfield, Michigan

Temple Shalom, Floral Park, New York, N.Y.

Temple Beth Shalom, Fredericksburg, Va.

Temple Isaiah of Lexington, Ky.

Beth Thorah, North Miami Beach, Fla.

Reform Temple of Putnam Valley, New York, N.Y.

Temple Shaare Tefilah, Norwood, Mass.

Neve Shalom Congregation of Belair Bowie, Md.

Temple Emanuel, Denver, Colorado

B'nai Judah Beth Elohim, Glenview, Ill.

Temple Emanuel Woolahra, New South Wales, Australia

LAST ENCOUNTER
PAVEL FANTEL

While examining new paintings in the archives of Yad Vashem art museum, I came across scenes depicting with sarcastic humor the daily life in Ghetto Terezín. I wondered to myself who this artist could be who not only had the talent but the guts to catch and sketch on paper the indignities suffered by the Jewish inmates of the ghetto for posterity?

These pitiful scenes show inmates sitting in public lavatories crammed next to one another, wistfully thinking of the luxury and privacy of their own lavatory in better days. Or paintings depicting the gradual deterioration of body and spirit.

The name Dr. Pavel Fantel rang a bell. I had to be sure. Out of the archives of Yad Vashem I pulled a list of Transport Aad from Kolin, Czechoslovakia, penalty transport for the assassination of Reinhard Heydrich, Reich Protector of Bohemia and Moravia, June 1942.

And then the memories started to come back...

One morning a messenger came to my grandmother's house, where my mother, sister and I were living after being thrown out of our home by the Nazis. The messenger was from the Jewish

*I am curious if the beautiful days when I was alone in the lavatory
will ever return!*

Pavel Fantel

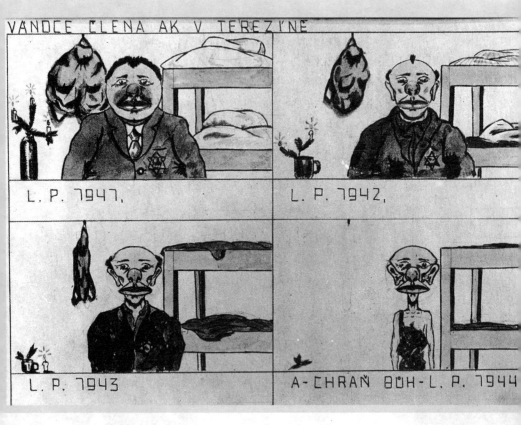

Hunger in Terezín   *Pavel Fantel*

community, with an order from the Gestapo Headquarters for me to present myself there immediately. My mother grew pale, fear gripped her whole being. Her child going to the Gestapo? Alone? What for... What has she done? Will she return? Ever?

In 1941, we Czech Jews were completely at the mercy of the German occupying forces and had no choice but to obey.

I put on clean underwear, slipped a toothbrush in my pocket, and parted from my mother with a few cheerful words trying to dissipate her fears, while mine were already taking hold of me.

By the time I reached the Gestapo Headquarters, I was paralyzed with fear. I had no idea why I was being sent for – and why me – of all the local Jews that were under the supervision of the local Gestapo.

I presented the note-order from the Gestapo to the sentry outside the heavily guarded building and waited for admission. There waited little me, with a Star of David sewn on the left side of my coat, its yellow color screaming out JEW, and I prayed as I had never prayed before.

At that moment I realized that I was not a child any longer. I became familiar with fear, a fear that didn't leave me for many years.

That is where I met Dr. Pavel Fantel, a former military doctor in the regular Czech army. In 1940, when Jews were forced to leave their places of residence and work, for whatever reason the Germans found justifiable at the time, Dr. Fantel moved to Kolin with his wife Marta, his mother, and his small son, Tomy.

We worked at the Gestapo in an index card complex, where every Jew from the whole district was identified by his particulars, a photograph, and a complete background history of his life and all of his activities to date. These were gathered by the many collaborators that the Germans recruited among the Czech population, many of them with greedy eyes on prospective Jewish property.

Dr. Fantel taught me how to destroy a card of a Jew who succeeded in escaping, so that no trace could be found. He taught me how to smuggle notes or a little food to Jews that were held at the Gestapo, how to get messages transmitted to people that had been arrested and not been heard from since.

Pavel Fantel was a slight, unimposing man – bright, intelligent, courageous and talented. His wonderful sense of humor helped sustain us during the difficult hours we spent together at the Gestapo.

We met again briefly in Terezín in an isolation building called Sokolovna, where I was a typhoid patient and he was a medical doctor in charge of the hospital. When time permitted, he would bring us news of what was happening outside of the ghetto walls. With his ingenuity, even in those difficult days, he found ways to keep in touch with the outside world.

According to his friend, Adi Löbl, whose portrait is among the collection of Fantel's paintings in Yad Vashem, these paintings were smuggled out of Ghetto Terezín prior to Fantel's departure for Auschwitz. They were hidden and kept by a Czech friend, who returned them, after the war, to Fantel's mother.

Dr. Pavel Fantel, his wife, and his son Tomy did not return from the camps. But his paintings are a reminder of the bravery of the individual and the spirit that could not be crushed under the horrible persecution by the Germans.

We Will Not Forget   *Pavel Fantel*

AS IF IT HAPPENED YESTERDAY

On October 7, 1942, while in Terezín, my mother, sister and I were scheduled to be included in a transport of 1,000 inmates leaving the ghetto for some unknown place in the East.

Expecting the worst, my mother, who worked as a nurse in the ghetto, injected herself and became deathly ill. In that way, she managed to get the three of us out of that particular transport. This saved our lives temporarily. That transport was sent to Treblinka and my cousin was its only survivor.

From him I heard of the horrors of Treblinka.

I have read about Treblinka. Yet when the trial started in Jerusalem – "Criminal Case Number 86, State of Israel versus Ivan (John), son of Nicolai Demjanjuk" – I felt compelled to attend.

Inside the packed courtroom, I listened to the proceedings. I pondered, as I had many times before, how the world is divided into two kinds of people: those who were there and those who were not.

The prosecutor could not understand what he was asking, and the words of the witnesses could not describe what they had lived through.

The witnesses were competent and calm most of the time, describing in words what they saw. But the horrors, the pain and the fear came through only at those rare moments when the survivors broke down, choking on their unspeakable memories.

Each day as I entered the courtroom, I forgot the world outside, for I entered the other world, a world forever living inside me, no matter where I am or how much time distances me from there. I entered the other world of barbed wire, bunk beds, *Appellplatz* (parade ground), prisoners' uniforms, blows and endless hunger. It all comes back as if it happened yesterday.

And I, who cannot remember where I put my glasses, where I left my keys, or the name of someone I met yesterday, remember

Treblinka

every night with the greatest clarity as I enter the other world, the places, the faces, the humiliations, and the pain.

And the next day, when I again sit in the courtroom listening to the civilized proceedings of a trial, conducted in a democratic country, listening to the defense counsel repeatedly asking the witness, "And what position were you in when you were looking at the *Schlauch* (a fenced-in pathway leading to the gas chamber), watching the poor wretches being driven into the gas chambers?," I dig my nails into my palms and bite my lips hard, because everything in me wants to SCREAM.

BACK FROM POLAND

This was my third and last trip to a country that represents the largest Jewish graveyard in the world.

Neither of my previous visits was a pleasure trip. The first was a journey into an inferno called Auschwitz-Birkenau. Alone, without my mother and father, I traveled with strangers in a sealed cattle-wagon. So close physically, yet lonely among so many. That was my first trip abroad from the country of my birth, Czechoslovakia, and I didn't need a passport, visa, or ticket. All that was taken care of by the Germans.

The second time I traveled to Poland was many years later, when for the first time I acquired a passport, could afford to pay for the trip, and found the time to travel.

Driven by a force that would not let me rest, I wanted to revisit and reconstruct the nightmares that had haunted me at night, and sometimes even in the daytime, for years. I wanted to see for myself what I had lived through then, locked in like an animal in a cage, not knowing where I was being sent, how I got there, what time of the day or night it was, what day of the week or which month of the year.

That time I traveled to Poland to confront the fear that lived within me. With my husband at my side, I flew to Warsaw, rode on a train for eight hours to Cracow, took a taxi to Auschwitz, and walked the three kilometers to Birkenau.

And there it was: the never-ending camps, the electric wire fences, the railway reaching all the way into the camp to the platform where selections of who would live and who would die were made. The guard post and one original barrack standing intact in a sea of hundreds of blackened chimneys reminded us of the vastness of the camp, of all the barracks once standing there.

We were alone then, not a soul around us. Most people are taken to Auschwitz, where the history of the Polish Holocaust is presented to them. Very few visitors know about, or are brought to, the Jewish section called Birkenau.

We searched and walked until we came to the remains of the gas chambers, blown up by the retreating Germans in January 1945. Only then did I realize how close I had been to them, when incarcerated in camp B2B in 1944. Yet I had no idea where they were and how they were operated.

We examined the ruins of these monstrous devices that devoured over two million people, human beings, Jews, my mother among them.

Emotionally drained, we got back to the waiting taxi, returned to Cracow, boarded a train and left Poland.

During the next ten years, having done research on different aspects of the Holocaust, speaking and working at Yad Vashem, I learned about Treblinka, Belzec, Chelm and Majdanek, about the Bialystok, Warsaw and Lodz ghettos, and of the full Jewish life of the three and a half million Jews in Poland before the Second World War.

My third trip to Poland was with a tour organized by Yad Vashem, covering some of the above-mentioned concentration camps. This time it was for me more of an academic venture to study the extent of the destruction of the Jews from all European countries under German occupation, that took place on Polish soil.

We first visited Treblinka, situated in a huge isolated field, with 17,000 broken stones, reminders of the destroyed communities. Its starkness and simplicity have a devastating effect.

Next stop was Majdanek, the one camp which remains almost as it was then. In its swift advance in the fall of 1944, the Russian army surprised the Germans, who had no time to destroy the evidence. Here the gas chambers are intact and could be reactivated any time – so chillingly real.

The third camp we saw was Auschwitz. With a special guide provided for our group, we spent three and a half hours in Auschwitz, hearing about the Polish Holocaust, the suffering of the Polish prisoners, the Polish uprising, Polish martyrdom. With the red brick Carmelite Monastery hovering over the camp and a large cross protruding high above the wall, stating in no uncertain terms who occupies this place, I asked our guide when we would get to the other part of Auschwitz, called Birkenau.

There were three Auschwitz survivors among our group. When we reached the ruins of the gas chambers, all three of us broke down and, holding on to each other, we cried. Each lit a candle of remembrance and said her own prayer. Then each tried to locate the exact camp where she had been housed while enslaved there. Everyone had come from a different place, arrived at a different time, lived in a different camp. Yet all three of us lived through the same Auschwitz experience, which played havoc with our lives for the rest of our days.

After Auschwitz, there was nothing more I wanted to see in Poland. A free day in Warsaw, and we were ready to leave this land soaked in Jewish blood.

As our group had a common visa, everything took a long time. Adding to the confusion, Warsaw's small airport had no English signs anywhere. Our luggage was finally weighed and we proceeded to the bus to take us to a small Lot airplane.

When everybody was seated, my name was called. It seems that in the rush and confusion at the airport, I omitted some formality that almost at any other airport would have been solved courteously within minutes.

Instead, I was taken off the plane and driven back to the terminal, where my passport and ticket were taken from me. I was told that I would not be allowed to proceed to Israel with my group.

And there I was, again alone in Poland, without a passport or a ticket, without money or friends, in a country that had no diplomatic relations with Israel, shouted at as if I were a criminal, about some foolish oversight in getting a custom stamp on my luggage.

Trying to keep calm, I used my wits and humor to extract myself from this very unpleasant situation. After an hour I was driven back to the plane that had been kept waiting on the runway all this time.

Back in my seat, headed for Israel, I realized that those of us who have a number branded on our arm, like a page of history that all the rubbing can never wash away – as a reminder of Auschwitz – we can neither forgive nor forget...

MURDER ON YOM KIPPUR

One sad day in 1943, the 24th of August, an order was received in Ghetto Terezín that all inmates were to remain in their present dwelling places, be it the old army *"Kaserne,"* large stone barracks, or the overcrowded houses, where 20 to 50 people lived in each room. No one was allowed to look out, even peep from a window, under the threat of severe punishment. Rumors circulated. In fear we asked ourselves: "What now? What new blow have the Germans thought of? What humiliation, what punishment awaited us this time? Another transport to the East? Did somebody succeed in escaping?"

Suddenly, a column of bedraggled children appeared, hundreds of them between the ages of four to twelve years, holding each other's hands. The older ones helped the small ones, their little bodies moving along in the pouring rain. A column of marching ghosts, with wet rags clinging to their emaciated bodies, accompanied by a large number of SS men.

Were these the enemies of the Third Reich to be so fiercely guarded? The children were led to a building where disinfection and delousing of inmates was performed. Suddenly they started to

◀ *Auschwitz*
Dinah Gottlieb

shout and cry: "Gas! Gas! Gas!" They huddled together, refusing to be washed or have their wet rags changed for dry clothing. Nobody understood the children's reaction. What kind of children are these? Where did they come from? What are they talking about?

The children, looking like scarecrows, refused to undress. They held on to their dirty clothing, the older stepping in front of the young ones, protecting them with their bodies, clutching their hands and comforting those that were crying. Their clothing permeated with lice, their bodies full of sores, these children refused to wash.

In 1943, we, the inmates of Ghetto Terezín, didn't know anything about gas chambers. Locked away, isolated from the outside world, we lived in fear and ignorance of what awaited us once we left the Ghetto, advertised by the Germans as *"Die Stadt die Hitler den Juden geschenkt hat."* ("The town which Hitler gave to the Jews.")

Prior to the children's arrival, there was a great deal of rushed work done outside the walls of the Ghetto, in a place called *Kreta*. A special group of male inmates, constantly accompanied by SS guards, was putting up wooden barracks for an unknown purpose.

With the Ghetto under strict curfew, the best doctors and nurses were picked out from among the inmates of Terezín, all those chosen having worked until then with children of the Ghetto in some capacity. They were rounded up and taken outside of the Ghetto walls to the newly erected barracks, to meet these strange children – that had arrived no one knew from where.

Food, clothing, and medicine were immediately delivered to the children, all under the supervision of the SS men. No one was allowed to talk to them. Yet as time went by, the children told their

The author with her mother

horror stories to the doctors and nurses, who, in time, defying German death threats, smuggled these stories back to the Ghetto. Sometimes they hid them in the utensils that brought their food to and from the Ghetto.

The children came from Bialystok Ghetto in Poland. They spoke Polish and Yiddish. They were terribly frightened and in a state of shock.

Our family had been sent to Terezín a year and a half earlier. We were a dwindling group. My father was sent away in a transport in 1942, as were my grandmother and aunt and many of my friends. My grandfather, knowing he was too old to survive the daily suffering, took his life. Only my mother, sister and I remained.

At Terezín, my mother worked as a nurse in a home for babies. She loved children and felt a deep need to care for those little creatures who could not understand why they did not receive enough food to still their hunger.

One day, when I returned from work, my sister told me that our mother had been removed outside the Ghetto that morning to work in the children's barracks. The move was so sudden that she had to leave her belongings behind and could take only a few things with her.

Only one thought then occupied my mind. How could I get to see my mother again?

Through a friend who was in charge of agriculture, I arranged to be included in a work crew growing vegetables for the Germans in the fields outside the Ghetto. The first day at work I observed the guards' movement and planned how to approach the children's barracks, which sat behind barbed wire on a hill separated from us by a moat. The next day, wearing a green sweater and a borrowed green skirt for camouflage, I watched the children's compound while I worked, until I saw my mother come out of the barracks. I waited until the guards were not looking my way, crawled to a clump of greenery facing the barracks and called out: "Mother, Mother!"

She could not see me. I called again: "It's I, Hana." She turned in the direction from which my voice was coming, and I asked how she was and what had the children told her.

"Terrible, terrible," she answered, "I cannot talk."

As she sat down on the grass in her white nurse's outfit, the children around her, her black hair framing her face, she was beautiful. That is the picture I carry of her in my mind. A guard drew near, and I crawled back to my work place without being discovered.

And then, one day, they all disappeared in the same way they had arrived. In the morning of the 5th of October, 1943, the wooden barracks at *Kreta* were empty. Again, through the Ghetto grapevine, we, the inmates, learned that all the doctors and nurses, on leaving the Ghetto in an exchange deal, had been ordered to remove the yellow stars Jews wore on every garment and had been forced to sign a pledge of silence as to what they had seen and lived through, and were on their way to Switzerland to be exchanged through the Red Cross for German prisoners of war.

From that moment my spirits soared. No matter how hard my life became, I believed that my mother was alive, in some safe place, and that we would be reunited after the war.

Six months later, I was transported with 5,000 others to Auschwitz. None of us was prepared for the visual horror and harsh treatment that greeted us there. When we asked what happened to the transports that arrived before us, there was a standard answer: "Up the chimney." I consoled myself that at least my mother wasn't there to witness the horror of Auschwitz.

Unknown to us, the prisoners of the Ghetto, their sentence had already been pronounced by their murderers.

Adolf Eichmann, influenced by strong protestation from the Mufti of Jerusalem, Haj Amin el Hussein, that these Jewish children would soon be adults reinforcing the Palestine Jewish community, cancelled the entire operation on express orders from S.S. chief Himmler.

And so, on Erev Yom Kippur, October 7, 1943, 1,196 children from Bialystok Ghetto in Poland, and 53 doctors and nurses from the Terezín Ghetto in Czechoslovakia, who accompanied them to the end, said their last *"Shema"* in the gas chambers of Auschwitz.

DOCUMENTATION

My quest to find out what happened to my mother began April 15, 1945, the day I was liberated from Bergen-Belsen. The search took me to the files and archives of the Red Cross, the United Nations, YIVO, the Joint Distribution Committee and Yad Vashem; to information centers in the U.S., Europe and Israel, and to many long interviews and arduous correspondence.

As soon as I returned to Prague, I began sending telegrams to the Red Cross in Switzerland, England and Sweden. The answer was always in the negative. They had never heard of a children transport from Terezín.

For some years, this remained the case. Although I witnessed that a large number of children had come to Terezín and were sent out again after six weeks of intensive rehabilitation, I had no evidence to prove that it actually happened.

1.   Finally, material about Terezín began appearing in publications. The first confirmation came in 1953 in a book by Zdenek Lederer, "Ghetto Terezín," which mentioned a transport of children accompanied by doctors and nurses, from Terezín to Auschwitz. Lederer wrote: "The Germans had pretended that this transport would be sent to Switzerland, but according to the evidence given

by prisoners working in Oswiecim, the whole transport was taken from the station to the gas chambers. Survivors – 0 (zero)."

Aside from an overstatement of the number of children – Lederer put it at 1,500 – the essence of the story appeared in those few lines. The issue of German motivation heightened the questions in my mind.

2. Two years later, H.G. Adler wrote in his book: 'Theresienstadt 1941-1945.' Tubingen 1955, published by J.C.B. Mohr, pages 54, 151, writes: "1,200 children were brought to Theresienstadt on 24th of August 1943. On Erev Yom Kippur, 7th of October 1943, transport Dn/a, consisting of 1,196 children and 53 adults, was sent to the gas chambers immediately upon arrival in Auschwitz. The children were originally from Bialystok. Their parents were shot during an uprising in the Ghetto in August 1943."

As the facts about the transport became more and more precise, I looked further for an explanation of what the Germans intended to do with the children and why the deal fell through. Eventually I accumulated details that fit together like pieces in a jigsaw puzzle.

3. On the tenth anniversary of the uprising in Ghetto Bialystok, historian Berl Mark wrote in Biuletin Lidovskiego Instytutu Historycnego, published by Kwiecien-Wrzesien, 1953, No. 2-3.

"Ten years have passed since the last of the Jewish people's tragedy in Bialystok. On August 16, 1943, Hitler's murderers entered the Bialystok Ghetto and with the help of tanks and artillery started the ultimate annihilation of the remaining 40,000 Jews. The most refined bestiality was applied to the elderly, to the sick and to the children.

"Babies were killed on the spot by crushing of their skulls on the walls. A transport of approximately 2,000 older children was sent to Theresienstadt Ghetto, where murderers in white coats used the children for medical experiments and their blood for transfusion to wounded German soldiers."

4. Zeszyty Oswiecimske, published by the museum in Auschwitz, reports: Copies of handwritten lists of transports arriving in

Auschwitz were found. One of the entries reads: "7.10.1943 RSHA transport brought from Ghetto Terezín camp 1,196 children together with doctors and nurses. They were disposed of the same day in the gas chambers."

5. Josef Lanik, prisoner No. 29162, who escaped from Auschwitz to warn the world, wrote in his book, "Co Dante nevidel" (What Dante didn't see), how he marked down all transports that arrived and were exterminated in Auschwitz, how many people, and exact date of gassing. In his records he also mentions: 7th October 1943, gassed 1,200 children and about 50 accompanying adults that were brought into the camp. Book published by Osveta-Bratislava, 1964, Czechoslovakia.

6. The testimony of Dr. Tuvia Citron, Yad Vashem Archives, M.M./B 165:

"On Tuesday, 17th of August 1943, the Bialystok Ghetto was in flames after an uprising was started by the Jews who were being deported out of the Ghetto to their annihilation in Treblinka. The SS selected 2,000 children, tearing them away from their parents. The Sienkiewicz Gymnasium, located opposite the Toz Hospital, was emptied and the children were brought in on orders of two Gestapo men, Friedel and his assistant Gibus.

"The wife of the head of the Judenrat, Mrs. Barash, brought me an order to prepare the gymnasium. I was in charge of the children for the next two days. Messrs. Bernstein and Mansach were also with the children.

"That same night the Germans began shooting into the Ghetto, including the building where the children were located. The bullets penetrated the windows of the building, hitting the children standing nearby. Many children were wounded, some were killed.

"On the 19th of August, the situation changed. Dr. Katznelson, a member of the Jewish council in Bialystok, replaced me. Mrs. Sprung, secretary of the Jewish council, and a few women were put in charge of the children. All contact between the Ghetto inmates and the children ceased.

"On Friday, August 20th, 1943, after the Germans suppressed the uprising, the children were taken in trains out of Bialystok."

7. The testimony of Andrew Steiner, architect-engineer from Tatranska Lomnice, Czechoslovakia, which I found at the YIVO Institute in New York City and in Yad Vashem archives M5-165, in Jerusalem:

"I was negotiating with the German Adviser for Jewish Affairs at the Slovak government, SS Hauptsturmführer Dieter Wisliceny, member of the German embassy in Bratislava. I was representing Jewish interests and as such was in constant contact with respective places in Switzerland and in Palestine...

"I suggested his [Wisliceny's] help for saving Jewish children from Poland. At first his reply was negative... I persisted until he promised to present the situation to Eichmann. Several weeks later he informed me that an action of this kind could be carried out in principle, providing we were prepared to pay a considerable sum in dollars and the delivery of certain consignments from Slovakia to Germany."

Steiner relates that he promised to meet all conditions in return for the release of 1,000 Jewish children to Palestine via Switzerland, taking it for granted that overseas Jewish sources would provide the dollars needed.

"The terrible disappointment cannot be described when we received the notification by the American Joint and by other Jewish agencies... that due to patriotic reasons they were unable to support... a plan to deliver large sums of dollars that would be equal to direct aid to the enemy."

According to Steiner, instead of notifying the Germans that the deal was falling through, he decided to stall in the hope of obtaining the money. He asked for proof of German readiness. An agreement was reached: an initial payment to the Germans when the children arrived at Terezín, the balance payable when the children entered Switzerland. Steiner added:

"One day Wisliceny informed me.. that the children had arrived in Terezín and asked me for the first payment... Unfortunately, an ill-applied sense of "correctness" won with our foreign partners and... the dollar payment was denied. I had no choice but to notify Wisliceny... whereupon the children, after several weeks' stay in Terezín – instead of traveling to beautiful Switzerland and to free Palestine – were sent to Auschwitz and into the gas chambers."
The testimony seems straightforward: no money, no children.

8. The testimony of Dieter Wisliceny on the 15th of July, 1946, Nuremberg trial documents, Yad Vashem, states:

"...at the end of 1942 I tried, at the request of a group, to persuade Eichmann and Himmler to stop exterminating European Jewry and to allow some Jewish children to emigrate to Palestine.

"I had already discussed with representatives of the Joint in Bratislava the possibility of allowing adults to accompany the transport and we even discussed the number. Later some of the children arrived in Theresienstadt.

"Eichmann then told me to report to him in Berlin. He told me there the matter had come to the notice of the Mufti through his intelligence service in Palestine. Haj Amin el-Husseini, the grand Mufti of Jerusalem, who spent the war in Berlin as guest of the Germans, has protested to Himmler against the scheme, giving as his reason that these Jewish children would be adults in a few years and would reinforce the Palestine Jewish community.

"According to Eichmann, Himmler cancelled the entire operation and even issued an order banning any future occurrences of this nature, so that no Jew would be allowed to go to Palestine from areas under German control."

Another possibility has been suggested. General Erwin Rommel, after the defeat of his Africa Corps at El-Alamein in 1943, returned to Germany and asked Hitler's approval of a deal to raise the morale of his troops by ransoming thousands of German soldiers captured by the British. The *quid pro quo* would have been Jews, particularly Jewish children, for German soldiers. Far-fetched as this may seem, it could tie in with the Mufti's learning of the Theresienstadt transport.

9. In an old age home in Israel I interviewed 87 year old Hadassa Lefkowitz, who as secretary to the head of the Bialystok Judenrat had been chosen to accompany the children out of Bialystok. Although she wrote an article about this episode in a Yiddish publication in 1948, no one had spoken to her about this incident until our meeting on October 23rd, 1987.

   Hoping to save one four year old girl, she pretended to be her mother. The Germans discovered the pretext, and instead of letting the child off the train at Terezín, sent them both to Auschwitz, where the little girl was immediately gassed. Because she knew five languages, Hadassa was put to work in an office at Auschwitz. Six weeks after her arrival she saw an index card noting that a transport of children had been given "special treatment." She knew that the Bialystok children were no more.

10. The Yad Vashem archives have obtained material from Ghetto Terezín. Among the documents was a list, *Abtransport* Dn/a 5.19.1943. It is complete with the names of 1,196 children, giving the date, place of birth, and names of both parents. Some families had three or four children in the transport. The oldest was fourteen and the youngest four years old. It could not be more clear, that this was the list of the Bialystok children.

THE HOLOCAUST
AND UNFINISHED MOURNING

The Holocaust and its history, no matter how often researched, remains a well of never ending discoveries. It was this constant search into the fate of the Bialystok children, as new facts came to light in the course of many years, that directed my attention to the problem of mourning.

My research paper on the fate of the Bialystok children tells about the murder on Yom Kippur, the holiest of the Jewish Holy Days, of 1,196 children from the Bialystok Ghetto in Poland. These children were brought by train from Bialystok to Terezín for six short weeks to await an exchange that never materialized. Instead they were sent with 53 accompanying adults from Terezín Ghetto to their death in Auschwitz. The paper about the fate of the Bialystok children was presented at the "Remembering for the Future" conference in Oxford, England, in 1988.

After the publication of my book, I received letters from children of those accompanying adults, their murdered parents.

These children never entered the camps and were never subjected to persecution. Yet, all of them had this yearning to express their pain, sorrow, loss and personal bereavement.

One day I received a call from Yad Vashem, that a young English doctor was inquiring about the fate of the Bialystok transport. Dr. Ivor Gach came from England to Israel in search of his father's fate. He knew that his father was interned in Terezín Ghetto. He knew his father was a part of some children's transport, and he knew that his father didn't return.

After reading my book *From Kolin to Jerusalem* he realized the story of the Bialystok children is his father's story. When we met eventually I gave him my research paper to read, with all pertinent documentation and the copy of the Dn *Abtransport* list, with his father's name and date of death.

Ivor came from a mixed marriage. His father divorced his mother to save his son. Ivor was brought up not knowing his father's fate. All he had was a photograph of his father and the last letter his father managed to smuggle out of the Ghetto, prior to his departure to an unknown destination. The letter hinted that he had been separated from the rest of the Terezín inmates, was leaving the Ghetto for a faraway place, and asked that his son say a prayer for him. (In Jewish religion a son says Kaddish for his dead father.)

Another letter that arrived at my publishers' office in Israel was from Prague, the Czech Republic. The letter was written by Hana Fousova, who received my book from her son as a Christmas present, because the Czech title "From Kolin to Jerusalem" caught his eye. His grandmother, Hana Fousova's mother, came from Kolin and therefore he thought the book might be of interest to his mother, without realizing the contents of the book.

And these are Hana's words:

> "When I was eight years old, I woke up one morning and mother was gone. My father who was not Jewish, died in 1940. Therefore my mother was no longer protected, according to the Nuremberg Laws,

by a mixed marriage. She was suddenly called up for deportation in the Kolin transport to Terezín in 1942."

Hana was left with the non-Jewish grandparents. She writes: "I was only eight years old when mother disappeared. I received a letter from her, prior to her departure from Terezín, a very optimistic one, telling me not to worry, that she is leaving for Switzerland. This letter was smuggled out by a Czech policeman, and because of the fear at that time that the courier might be discovered, my grandmother always burned all evidence."

New year greeting made in Terezín by one of the Bialystok children for Emily Reinwald in 1943

In her last letter the mother, Emilie Reinwald, included a doll made by the Bialystok children and a greeting card for Rosh Hashana, the Jewish New Year, that one of the children, Mojzse Treszczanski, whose name I traced on the transport list of the Bialystok children, wrote and decorated for her. It is written in German, probably the only language they had in common, with grammatical mistakes. This little card with good wishes Hana hid from her grandmother, and today it is **the only known evidence** that remained of the 1,196 children who met their death in the Auschwitz gas chambers on the eve of 'Yom Kippur 1943.'

In this last letter the mother sends warm greetings to her daughter for her 9th birthday and regrets that it is going to be without mother or father. Interesting to note, there is a request to her daughter to go to the cemetery and lay a bunch of flowers on her father's grave, to observe a "Jahrzeit" in spite of the fact that the father was not Jewish.

After the velvet revolution in Prague, when my book was published in Czech, I received a call from the daughters of Otilia David, sister of Franz Kafka, the famous Czech writer.

Helena Rumpoldova and Vera Soudkova were two other children who didn't know their mother's fate. Otilia David insisted on divorcing her husband, so that he would save their two daughters, Helena and Vera, from deportation to Terezín. Otilia David became one of the accompanying nurses of the children's transport.

When I asked Helena, what did she do when her mother was deported, she replied: "I prayed and cried for a year." For forty years they didn't know their mother's fate until the publication of my book in Czech, in Prague.

What I found was common to all these children whose parents were murdered was that it left an open wound all these years, a wound that had no chance to heal. There was no finality, no precise knowledge, no place of burial and no answers to their questions.

Because these children were brought up outside the Jewish community, they lacked the ability to make contact with the community of survivors, who might have helped them to discover at least some facts which in any case, in the turmoil of the aftermath of the war and lack of adequate communications, was difficult at best.

Now these children, whose parents were murdered, have been able to begin the process of mourning by having a definite date, place and other information on what happened. They finally found something tangible to relate to.

What is the procedure that takes place when someone dies in the family? In the Jewish religion, we sit *Shiva*, which means in translation, seven days of mourning. The custom is for the bereaved family to take time off from its daily routine and, after the funeral, to sit together, usually in the home of the departed one, wearing soft shoes and ripped clothing, talking about the dead person. Comforting each other, crying together, saying prayers. Friends, colleagues, neighbors come to participate in our sorrow and express their sympathy.

They offer help, bring food, so the bereaved can devote all their time to mourning, contemplation and eventually relief. After a week, the family gets up and returns to the routine of daily life. There was pain, there was a funeral, a grave, a time to mourn and remember and then life continues. Each year on the anniversary of the death, "Jahrzeit," a day of remembering is observed, by lighting a candle, visiting the grave, and a special prayer for the dead, "Kadish," is recited.

The situation with the bereaved of Holocaust victims is entirely different. People were killed, murdered, gassed, tortured to death,

Emilie Reinwald

Marie Lustig

Dr. Leo Gach

Otla Kafka-David

shot. There were no bodies, no funerals, no graves, no prayers. A total void filled with pain, and no mourning time.

Here are some examples of how survivors mourn the dead:

1. Sometimes when a survivor is attending the funeral of somebody not even close, he will cry, not for the person being buried but for those that were never buried.
2. When visiting Auschwitz-Birkenau some years ago, three survivors crawled inside the gas chambers, as macabre as it may sound, to scrape some ashes to take home with them.
3. On the fiftieth anniversary of the liberation of Auschwitz, thousands of survivors dragged themselves to Auschwitz, to this horrible, cursed place, to mourn, to cry, to remember – for they have no other place to go.
4. In the Jewish religious calendar, there is a special date for those whose date of death is not known.

Because of my research, the following people have found solace in establishing the date and place of their parents.

Ivor Gach, son of Dr. Leo Gach, b. 25.12.1891.

Vera and Helena David, daughters of Otla Kafka-David, b. 21.6.1906.

Hana Fousova, daughter of Emilie Reinwald, b. 7.6.1904.

Irena and Hana Lustig, daughters of Marie Lustig, b. 16.4.1902.

EPILOGUE

1. When Memory Comes...

I never knew that Dr. Pavel Fantel had a brother, we never spoke of personal matters. It was while I was invited to speak in Northwood and Pinner Liberal Synagogue in London, a recipient of one of the Kolin Tora scrolls, that someone from the audience approached me to tell me about Fantel's brother. He escaped in time from Czechoslovakia and achieved a magnificent record as a flier with the R.A.F. He received the Czech War Cross, the

Dr. Pavel Fantel

Czech Order of Merit and the Order of the British Empire for his bravery.

It took another 10 years before my book reached Fantels' brother through his cousin, living in Eilat. I received a wonderful letter from this 92 year old man, that I have translated here for the reader:

Dear Hana,

My cousin Miriam sent me your book and your address. I would like to thank you. You are the only one that put up a well deserved monument for my brother. Your words are warmer and more honest than the rehabilitating document or the promotion to Colonel that he received from the Czech authorities.

I admire you, my cousin and all the other young girls, whose youth was stolen, the loveliest part of one's life.

Pavel was my best friend, my colleague, critic and moral support. He wasn't so crazy and gypsylike as I, rather he was solid, reliable, intransigent in all his actions. My Pavel was shot in Silesia someplace near Hirschberg on the day of his 42nd birthday, the 7th of January 1945.

In gratitude and with many thanks,

Yours, Ernst Fantel,
Konstanz

2. Pen-Pals

When I visited Israel for the first time in 1950, I tried to find Michael Mahler's sister, who made aliya in 1939 from Czechoslovakia. That was all the information in my possession at that time. I asked wherever I went, and whenever I met people who had come before the war to Palestine from Czechoslovakia, but never found her.

Many years later I had a call from a friend, who after reading my book, told me she was from the same town as Michael, and that she knows his married sister, a member of Kibbutz Neot Mordechai in the Galilee. I immediately contacted her and we met. She confirmed what an exceptionally talented boy Michael was, writing poetry from early age in Czech, English and Hebrew. I was able to give her an account about the last days of Michael's life. She gave me a snapshot of Michael the way I remembered him, that she had taken with her to Palestine when she left home.

Michael Mahler

3. Art as Evidence

Unique evidence in Holocaust history are five paintings, drawn by different artists on the same day, depicting the procession of the Bialystok children walking through Terezín. Unaware of each other, these artists drew the children's arrival, each recording this unusual event in his own style.

One is by Ernest Morgan, a lawyer living in Australia who was a Ghetto Wachmann in Terezín. He painted out of a need to record, and never painted again. Immediately after the liberation, Morgan reconstructed and painted all the impressions he had drawn in Terezín and which were later lost in Auschwitz. All of this he donated to the Yad Vashem Art Museum in Jerusalem. His portrayal is of tired looking children in oversized old clothing, accompanied by Czech policemen and a few Ghetto Wachmänner, with stars on their coats. In the background we see a blocked street with people standing and watching the transport pass by, while all the windows in all the houses are closed tight.

Otto Unger was a professional painter, a well known artist and an art teacher in Brno prior to the war. He was seized for painting the gradual degradation of the inmates of the ghetto and was sent to the Small Fortress, Gestapo Headquarters, where his wife and daughter were also interned under terrible conditions. Unger died from typhus and exhaustion in Buchenwald, a month after liberation.

According to Leo Haas, his paintings were found buried under the floor in one of the barracks in Terezín. Other paintings by Fritta, Fleishman and Unger, hidden between two walls in Terezín, were also found after the war, unharmed.

Children transport, Terezín 1943   *Pavel Fantel*

Children transport, Terezín 1943   *Ernest Morgan*

Children transport, Terezín 1943   Otto Unger

Children transport, Terezín 1943   Leo Haas

Unger's painting depicts the ghetto walls, the children carrying small packages, and a nurse in a white uniform leading the column, while a policeman is marching alongside.

The third painting is by Pavel Fantel, doctor and a former major in the Czech army, who because of his expertise in bacteriology became the head of Sokolovna Children's isolation hospital for typhus patients, immediately upon his arrival in Terezín. Dr. Fantel was shot on a death march in Hirschberg, Silesia, in January 1945. Fantel was a talented amateur satirist and a caricaturist. Painting was his hobby.

Fantel's paintings were smuggled out from Terezín prior to his deportation to Auschwitz in October 1944 and hidden in Prague. They are today part of the Yad Vashem art collection in Israel.

His painting is of dark, misty figures, hardly discernible. Only the children's faces, without features, are like small lights shining in the night. The street is deserted, the column is headed by a Ghetto Wachmann, followed by an S.S. man whose S.S. cap is prominent.

The drawing by Leo Haas I discovered in a catalogue of the Sotheby auction house in Israel, in 1997, a drawing that had not been seen before in public and was untitled. It was sold with three other drawings from Terezín by Leo Haas, to an anonymous collector.

The drawing shows the Terezín style barracks, a tree without leaves in the background, many faces looking at the children's transport from behind closed windows. It depicts the large figure of a soldier with a gun towering over a group of tiny children in oversized clothing, being led by a person from the disinfection department, clad in a white overall.

The fifth, childish drawing is by Helga Hoskova, made on the 24th of August 1943 on her third floor bunkbed, from where she could see the children walking in the street accompanied by a policeman, while a Ghetto Wachmann, arms spread out, with a yellow star and Wachmann's hat, is preventing people behind him coming closer to the children walking by. Especially touching is 14 year old Olga's portrayal of an older boy holding a little girl's hand protectively, probably his younger sister.

The horror that strikes us from all five paintings is how heavily guarded were these parentless, frightened children.

As a result of my research into the fate of the Bialystok children I was able to identify these paintings. Today Morgan's and Fantel's paintings of the Bialystok children are exhibited at Yad Vashem, while Otto Unger's is in my private collection.

These paintings are the unique material evidence of the Bialystok children's fate in the history of the Holocaust.

Children's transport, Terezín 1943   *Helga Hoskova, 14 years old*

Shoah Continued...

My mother, who was married in 1922 in Kolin, in what was then Czechoslovakia, by a Rabbi, Dr. Richard Feder, later chief Rabbi of the Czechoslovak Republic, was divorced from my father in a civil ceremony in 1937, in the same town.

In 1939, when Czechoslovakia was occupied by the Germans, my father was banished from our town, while my sister and I continued to live with mother in grandmother's house, after being evicted from our home.

On the 10th of June 1942, as a penalty for the assassination of Reinhard Heydrich, our town was cleared of Jewish inhabitants and a train with 1,050 people was sent in the direction of Poland. At the Bohusovice station, 50 people were taken out of the train, the order being that only 1,000 Jews were to be killed as a reprisal. Therefore, the remaining 50, mother, sister and I among them, were sent walking to Ghetto Terezín, 3 km away.

Shortly after our arrival at the Ghetto, father was included in a transport and deported to Maly Trostinec in Poland, where he and 998 people traveling with him were killed immediately upon arrival, according to the testimony of one of the two survivors, Hanus Muntz, who told me the sad tale when I met him many years later in Prague.

In Terezín, my mother met a very nice man from Vienna by the name of Rudi Ehrlich. Mother told us that her friend was a lawyer for the well-known firm of Julius Meinel, which at the time had stores in many European countries, including Austria and Czechoslovakia. As times were very difficult and one never knew what the next day would bring, mother and her friend decided to marry. But that wasn't so simple. The Ghetto was under Jewish leadership, circumcision, marriage and divorce were conducted according to Jewish Law, not that there were many of these events in the Ghetto.

To their consternation, mother and her friend Rudi found that, since my mother wasn't divorced under Jewish law, she could not remarry, and my father was no longer there to correct that. Mother and Rudi continued their friendship until my mother was included in a children's transport and sent to the gas chambers of Auschwitz on Erev Yom Kippur, 7th October 1943.

Mother's friend Rudi remained in the Ghetto, visited us whenever there was an opportunity, and was a great source of comfort to us, as we were alone.

Soon after, transports started leaving the Ghetto and this time Dr. Rudi Ehrlich was included. When he came to say goodbye to me and my sister, he handed us two pieces of paper with his signature, powers of attorney, as he had no other relatives. One was for food parcels that he was receiving in the Ghetto from a non-Jewish friend in Vienna, with whom he left a considerable amount of money. That was allowed from time to time. The other was for the sum of four million German marks that he had deposited in a numbered account in Switzerland prior to his departure for Terezín. We stayed with him all night until the train left and never saw him again.

Soon after, it was my fate to be part of a transport, whose destination, unbeknown to us, was Auschwitz. When I parted from my sister, naturally she kept the power of attorney for the parcels that were supposed to arrive in Terezín. In fact, they arrived half empty, if delivered at all.

Among the few possessions that were left to me after my stay in the Ghetto and which we were allowed to take with us, there was a leather container which was a former cigar holder. There I kept the few documents that remained. My birth certificate, the receipt from Gestapo for the jewelry that was confiscated from our family, my father's passport, my mother's photograph and my new acquisition, a power of attorney for four million German marks in a numbered Swiss account.

Upon arrival at our destination, Auschwitz, we were pushed by blows and frightened by shouts to evacuate the stinking overcrowded wagon that brought us there. All of our possessions were taken from us except for what we were wearing. I was holding on to my cigar container.

After a few weeks, five hundred women were selected from our camp for slave labor in Germany. Knowing that the selections were made while we were naked, I buried my leather container at night behind our barrack in a hole I dug up with my fingers, while watching the chimneys burning with the new arrivals of Hungarian Jews.

We left Auschwitz in our new sack uniforms, wooden clogs, tattooed like cattle, after the strictest examination of all parts of our bodies.

Worked and starved to death in the next year of slave labor in Hamburg, Germany, many times I thought how gladly I would trade the four million German marks for a single loaf of bread.

SURVIVORS BREAK THE SILENCE

The war ended and the concentration camps were opened. The people that inhabited those awful places and managed to stay alive through years of humiliation were freed. But were they? The freedom they had anticipated, for which they had fought to stay alive, was an illusion, for the reality of the world they had to face wasn't the same one they had left behind.

That world was shattered. It no longer existed. They could not return to the countries in which they were born – for political and other reasons. The homes they grew up in were non-existent. The fiber of the family unit was destroyed, the family members brutally murdered. The population amongst which they had grown up did not stand up for them when they were taken away by the Germans to concentration camps; those people could no longer be trusted.

The world, the western world, in which they had placed their confidence and their hopes, forgot them soon after the war was won and the shock over the horrors of the camps abated. Instead, what the word "freedom" meant to the survivors was very unrealistic in the realm of the political world of 1945.

No one waited for us – the survivors. There were no flowers, no celebrations, no bottles of champagne toasting our very survival. Instead there were D.P. (displaced persons) camps, Cyprus camps, long lines at different embassies and consulates, of people trying to rebuild their destroyed lives wherever the world would let them. Most countries were not interested. And so the survivors had to go about picking up the pieces wherever and in whichever way they could. It was not an easy task.

Most survivors were not well equipped to start a new existence. The majority were young people – old ones had been killed or didn't survive the harsh realities of a prisoner's daily life. They lacked education, professions, academic qualifications. The health of many was also damaged. They had no money and no one to support them – as in a normal family. Many of them lacked even the language with which to function, as survivors moved from country to country.

The fight for economic survival took precedence above all. People had to go to work, to make a living to eat.

The problems were immense. The loneliness, the lack of family support, the lack of moral support. The accents that accompanied them wherever they lived, the lack of a normal lifestyle – having friends from school, clubs, army, universities, communities. The difficulty of entering new societies with which they had no common language. Many survivors that came to Israel experienced feelings of separateness from the local population.

The survivors, carrying their background like a piece of luggage on their backs, were different. They thought differently, they felt differently, and they could not talk, for their language was not understood, and if it was, they immediately became a sensation, an object of pity, or were looked down upon.

Many could not accept the new freedom and ended their lives. Others fought like tigers to stay alive and build new lives for themselves, never mentioning their past to anybody. Very few entered academic life. That required financial support during studies, and long years before one could become independent. In spite of that, some managed to overcome even these obstacles. Most survivors went to work for a living. They worked hard, they married, had children and stayed silent.

Some wrote books or stories when they no longer could keep the horrors within themselves. Some of what they wrote was published, some was not, perhaps because the public was no longer interested. Some told their families, some could not even do that. And yet, most of the survivors had a tremendous need to tell, some had promised themselves, if they survived, it was their duty to tell. Some promised others who didn't survive to carry their message.

And then, in the sixties, Israel caught one of the major Nazi criminals, Adolf Eichmann, and brought him to trial. It was a turning point in the lives of the survivors. Suddenly they were called to be witnesses in front of the entire world; it became legitimate to tell...and the silence began to break.

Having attended the Eichmann trial, and meeting and listening to other survivors, I realized that my feelings of despair, fear, disillusion, loneliness and the need to tell were shared by so many others with a similar past. I was not abnormal or mentally deranged. Simply, my life was shattered and I need not be ashamed of my feelings.

Once that silence was broken, survivors were no longer looked upon as sheep going to slaughter. Stories of unprecedented heroism became known through research and personal accounts. The Holocaust became a subject to be studied and accepted.

Suddenly, survivors were in demand in schools, army units, learning institutions. Few were prepared for the task. Language difficulties, fear of breaking down while describing their suffering, lack of self-confidence – all were ample reasons to keep the survivor from speaking in public.

And I – I started very hesitatingly, first in the children's school, terrified that I might not be able to go through with it. I prepared slides on the Holocaust, accompanied by my explanations. Because of questions from the audience, I saw the need for wider knowledge of the subject, and slowly I started to study the Holocaust. I voraciously read all literature connected with the

Pencil Drawing   *Unknown Artist*

Holocaust, to be more knowledgeable and informative and to give dimension to my personal story.

While travelling and speaking to Jewish and non-Jewish audiences, I saw how important it was to bear witness. Meeting many survivors from various countries and different camps, I learned that every story was different, that the Holocaust had many faces, many of them still unknown. As much as we already knew, so much was still untold. And the survivors are the last people that can tell.

I created a program for teaching, coaching and directing survivors, eye witnesses to the Holocaust, how to present their experiences in public for educational purposes. It was based on personal experience, research, acquaintance with many survivors, and years of experience of practical implementation in different educational institutions to various audiences.

The program I prepared is a one-week seminar study for survivors only. Every day begins with an academic lecture on the background of the Holocaust, on different subjects related to European anti-Semitism: Unique and Universal Aspects of the Holocaust; The Bystanders; How the World Reacted to the Holocaust; and The Implications of the Holocaust for Jews and Christians; etc.

Two hours of workshop-speaking techniques: every participant must stand up in front of the class and speak for five to eight minutes about an incident he lived through. This is videotaped and played back later for open discussion.

Films and documentaries about the Holocaust are shown and discussed: Genocide, Ambulance, Warsaw Ghetto, and others.

By using Yad Vashem exhibits as part of the teaching process, we achieve great success. Success in this case means that we assist hundreds of survivors to be able to bear witness in public.

They gain confidence in their own ability to present their stories in public in a coherent and dignified way. Time marches on; today the youngest of the survivors are in retirement. They have more time to devote to public causes, they are financially more independent, and as memories are returning, it is also very therapeutic for the survivor to go out and tell...fulfilling a promise he or she made but only now has the chance to carry out.

IN APPRECIATION

I take this opportunity to express my gratitude to my husband, Murray Greenfield, for his love, understanding and continuous support in all my endeavors.

To my daughter, Meira Partem, who gave me confidence in my ability to learn; and to my sons, Dror and Ilan, for helping me in any and every way.

To my dear friend, Ruth Siegel, who has always been there to assist; and to all my other friends for their moral support throughout the years.

To Yad Vashem for giving me permission to use their archives.

Hana Greenfield

Typesetting: Marzel A.S. – Jerusalem
Cover Design: Studio Paz, Jerusalem

ISBN 965 229 185 4

Edition 9 8 7

Gefen Publishing House Ltd.	Gefen Books
POB 36004	12 New Street
Jerusalem 91360, Israel	Hewlett, NY 11557, USA
972-2-5380247	516-295-2805
E-mail: isragefen@netmedia.net.il	

Printed by Helma v.o.s. Prague

**Distributed by Jan Kanzelsberger,
Jana Masaryka 56, 120 00 Praha 2**

Send for our free catalogue

Library of Congress Cataloging-in-Publication Data
Greenfield, Hana.
Fragments of memory: from Kolin to Jerusalem / Hana Greenfield. – Rev. ed.
    p.   cm.
ISBN: 965-229-185-4
1. Jews—Persecution—Czech Republic—Kolin. 2. Holocaust, Jewish (1939-1945)— Czech
Republic—Kolin—Personal narratives. 3. Greenfield, Hana. 4. Holocaust
survivors—Biography. 5. Kolin (Czech Republic)—Ethnic relations. I. Title.
DS135.C96K655   1998
940.53'18'094371—dc21   98-9370
                                                                                   CIP